Popcorn Plants

by Kathleen V. Kudlinski
photographs by Jerome Wexler

 Lerner Publications Company • Minneapolis, Minnesota

For everyone who loves popcorn as much as I do. —KVK

Photographs reproduced with permission of: pp. 5, 13, © David Frazier/AGStock; p. 7, © B.W. Hoffmann/AGStock; p. 8, © Dan Guravich/Photo Researchers Inc.; p. 10, © Bryan Peterson/AGStock; p. 21, © Scott Sinklier/AGStock; pp. 24, 39, © Frank S. Balthis; pp. 34, 40, © Lynn M. Stone; p. 37, © Archive Photos; p. 42, © Independent Picture Service.

Illustrations on pp. 12, 22, 30 by Laura Westlund, © Lerner Publications Company.

Thanks to our series consultant, Sharyn Fenwick, elementary science/math specialist. Mrs. Fenwick was the winner of the National Science Teachers Association 1991 Distinguished Teaching Award. She also was the recipient of the Presidential Award for Excellence in Math and Science Teaching, representing the state of Minnesota at the elementary level in 1992.

Early Bird Nature Books were conceptualized by Ruth Berman and designed by Steve Foley. Series editor is Joelle Goldman.

website address: www.lernerbooks.com

Library of Congress Cataloging-in-Publication Data

Kudlinski, Kathleen V.
    Popcorn plants / by Kathleen V. Kudlinski ; photographs by Jerome Wexler.
       p. cm. — (Early bird nature books)
    Includes index.
    Summary: Describes the life cycle of the popcorn plant from the time the farmer plants the seed until the kernel explodes.
    ISBN 0-8225-3014-7 (alk. paper)
    1. Popcorn—Juvenile literature. 2. Popcorn—Life cycles—Juvenile literature. [1. Popcorn.] I. Wexler, Jerome, ill.
II. Title. III. Series.
SB191.P64K83 1998
635'.677—DC21   97-1122

Manufactured in the United States of America
1 2 3 4 5 6 – SP – 03 02 01 00 99 98

Contents

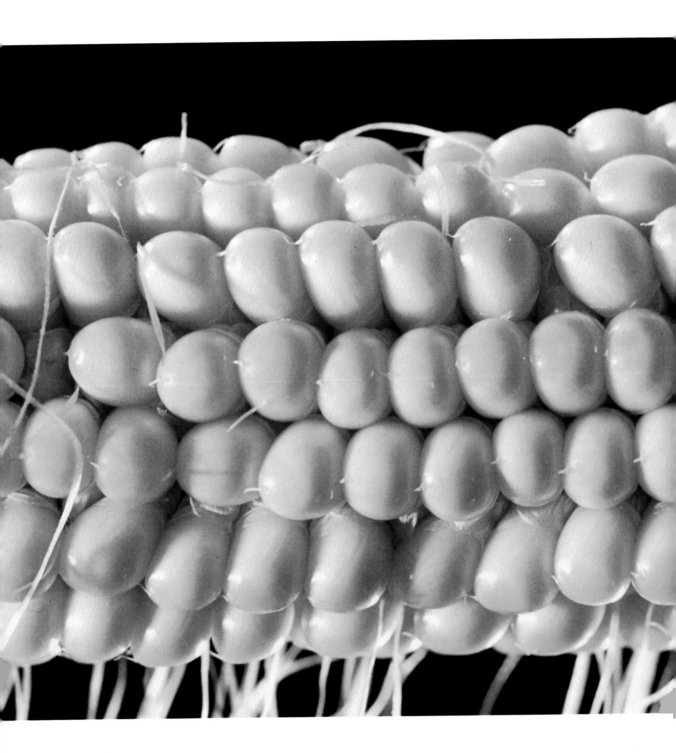

Be a Word Detective

Can you find these words as you read about the popcorn plant's life? Be a detective and try to figure out what they mean. You can turn to the glossary on page 46 for help.

carbon dioxide	minerals	pollinated
chlorophyll	nodes	stalks
corn silk	ovules	starch
hybrid	pollen	tassel

People all over the world eat popcorn. Popcorn plants once grew wild. Do popcorn plants still grow wild?

What Is Popcorn?

A pot of popcorn sits on the stove. Popping sounds fill the kitchen. When every kernel blows up into a big tasty puff, the popcorn is done. It smells so good, you can't wait to eat it.

Popcorn isn't made in a factory. It is a seed made by a popcorn plant. Popcorn plants used to grow wild. But there is no wild popcorn now. It is planted and grown on farms.

Popcorn is grown around the world. The middle of the United States is called the "corn belt." It is called the corn belt because this area is where most of the country's corn is grown.

The United States grows more corn than any other country. This farm is in Wisconsin. Wisconsin is a state in the "corn belt."

Corn comes in different shapes and sizes. From left to right, these ears of corn are called dent corn, sweet corn, flint corn, and popcorn.

There are many kinds of corn. Sweet corn is tasty and tender. We eat it right off the cob. Dent corn is the kind cows and pigs eat. It grows as tall as a school bus and has huge ears. Flint corn is sometimes fed to animals. People eat flint corn, too. Flour corn is the kind we grind into flour for tortillas (tor-TEE-yuhz) and corn chips. Indian corn has kernels that are different colors. There are many other kinds of corn, too. But only popcorn kernels pop up big and fluffy.

When a corn cob's kernels are different colors, we call the corn Indian corn. It is so pretty, we use it for decoration.

Corn grows next to oats in this field. Corn and oats are both grasses.

Popcorn and other kinds of corn are grasses. Wheat, rice, rye, oats, and sugarcane are grasses, too. Most people eat foods made from these grasses every day.

Most grasses have long, hollow stems called stalks (STAWKS). Corn stalks are different. They have a starchy filling inside. Starch is a food made by plants.

The filling inside corn stalks makes them stronger than most other grasses.

tassel

kernels

ear

node

husk

stalk

ear
(inside
husk)

silk

husk

leaf

Parts of a
Corn Plant

roots

A popcorn plant can grow to be six feet tall.

A popcorn stalk is bright green. It is about as thick as the base of a person's thumb. Its leaves are long and pointed. But the leaves are soft, so they flutter in the wind. Leaves grow all along the stalk. At the top of the stalk, a bunch of honey-colored strings blows in the wind. Here and there along the stalk are ears of popcorn.

Chapter 2

*Popcorn plants start
as seeds. When do
farmers plant
popcorn?*

Popcorn Grows

In the spring, a popcorn farmer plants popcorn kernels in a field. Then the farmer covers the kernels with soil. Kernels are the seeds of a corn plant. A kernel doesn't pop when it is planted. It grows.

The planted seed soaks up water from the soil. This makes the kernel swell up. Its hard coat softens. Three to five days later, the seed's coat splits. One tiny white root pushes down into the soil. The next day, a small white sprout breaks through the coat. The sprout grows upward.

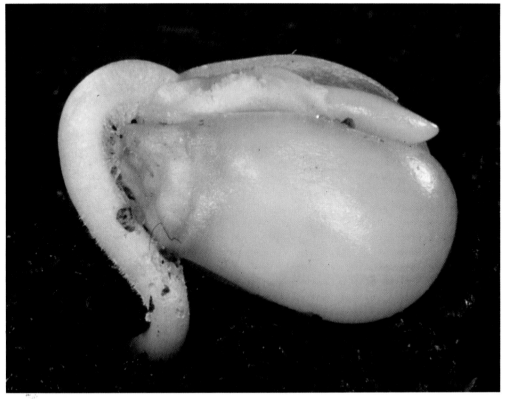

A kernel sprouts in moist soil.

In another day or two, more roots grow from the seed. The roots are covered with hairs. The root hairs soak up water from the soil. Then the water goes into the root and up into the sprout. The sprout pushes up through the soil. When it breaks through the dirt and out into the sunlight and air, the sprout turns green. It grows taller. Then it is called a stalk.

Tiny root hairs grow along each of a popcorn plant's roots.

Roots are important for all plants. Roots help popcorn plants grow.

Young popcorn plants have many roots and root hairs that take water from the soil. The roots grow about 1 foot deep. They are not very strong. If the wind blows hard, these roots may not be able to hold the stalk up.

Extra roots grow into the ground from the sides of a popcorn plant's stalk.

As the plant grows, extra roots sprout from the sides of the stalk near the ground. These roots look like fingers holding the plant up to the sunshine.

As soon as the plant pokes out of the ground, leaves sprout from the stalk. Popcorn leaves grow from special thick places along the stalk. These thick spots are called nodes. Nodes grow like rings around the stem. The first leaf grows from the first node. The next leaf grows from the next node on the other side of the stalk. As the plant grows taller, leaves keep growing in a zigzag pattern. The bottom of each leaf is wrapped around the stalk. The leaves hug the stalk tightly. This helps to make the stalk strong, so the plant can keep growing.

The popcorn plant's scientific name is Zea mays everta. Zigzagging leaves help to make a popcorn plant's stalk strong.

Chapter 3

Young popcorn plants need food to grow. What does a popcorn plant use for food?

Food for the Plant

All plants need food to grow. Starch and sugars inside the seed are the baby popcorn plant's food. Once the plant reaches the sunshine, it has used up the food in the seed. It needs a different kind of food. The growing plant uses sunlight to make its own food. It makes the food from water, air, and minerals (MIN-ur-uhls). Minerals are things that come from the soil.

Minerals from the soil go into the plant's roots with water. There are tiny tubes inside a corn plant's roots. The tubes go up through the stalk and into the tips of the leaves. Water and minerals travel all the way up the plant's tubes. The plant drinks them up, like you would suck soda through a straw.

When it rains, water soaks into the soil. A corn plant pulls the water from the soil with its roots.

Air is all around a popcorn plant. Air also moves through the plant. All over the bottom of each popcorn plant leaf are tiny holes. The holes are smaller than a pinprick. Air moves in and out through these holes. The part of air that plants use is called carbon dioxide (dy-AHK-side).

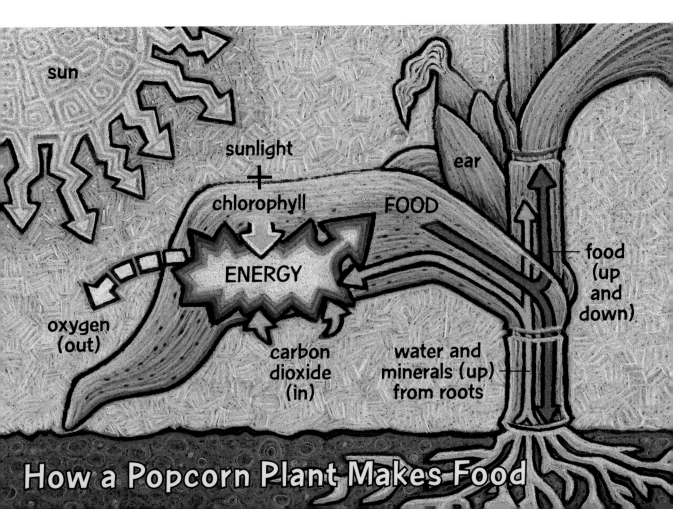

How a Popcorn Plant Makes Food

Chlorophyll makes popcorn leaves bright green.

Corn plants have something called chlorophyll (KLOR-uh-fihl) inside them. Chlorophyll is bright green. It gives plants their green color. It also makes food for plants. Chlorophyll uses the energy of the sun shining on the plant's leaves and stalk. With this energy, chlorophyll turns water, minerals, and carbon dioxide into food and a gas called oxygen (AHKS-uh-jihn). The plant uses the food to grow healthy and strong.

Chapter 4

All grass plants have flowers. How many kinds of flowers does a popcorn plant have?

Flowers

Imagine a bunch of flowers. You are probably thinking of bright, pretty flowers. But some flowers aren't pretty. Plants do not grow flowers so you can enjoy them. They grow flowers because flowers make seeds.

All grass plants grow flowers. Grass flowers do not have pretty colors. They do not smell good. They do not even look much like flowers, but they still make seeds.

Every popcorn plant has two kinds of flowers. One is a male flower. The other is a female flower. Together the two kinds of flowers make new kernels of popcorn.

The male flower grows at the top of a popcorn plant.

The yellow powder inside these sacs is pollen.

The male flower grows on top of the plant during the middle of summer. The male flower is called a tassel (TASS-uhl). It is a bunch of stiff honey-colored strings. Along these strings are hundreds of tiny pouches, called sacs. Each sac holds hundreds of grains of pollen. Pollen is a yellow powder.

A popcorn plant's female flowers are called ears. They grow in the cracks between the leaves and stalk. These flowers are shaped like fingers. They look like tiny ears of corn. Rows of bumps called ovules (AHV-yools) cover the ear. Ovules are baby seeds. A layer of special leaves covers each ear and its seeds. These leaves make up the husk. The husk keeps hungry insects, birds, and mice from eating the ovules. Threads called corn silk stick out from the top of the husk.

Small ears grow on popcorn plants by the middle of summer.

For the ovules to grow into kernels, pollen from a tassel must travel to the ear. Corn silk helps the pollen get to the ovules. Each soft, silky thread leads to one ovule.

One ear of corn has hundreds of strands of silk. Each strand of corn silk is attached to one ovule, or baby kernel.

The sacs on the tassels open and pollen falls out.

When the ovules are ready to grow, the silk on the ear becomes sticky. This happens at the same time that the tassel's pollen sacs open up. Wind blows through the tassel and shakes out thousands of grains of pollen. Clouds of pollen drift downward. Some pollen falls straight down onto the plant's ears. Some pollen drifts on the breeze and blows away.

How a Corn Plant is Pollinated

Wind can carry pollen from the tassel to the ear. Pollen can land on the silk of the corn stalk it came from or on the silk of a different stalk.

When a grain of pollen lands on the tip of a strand of silk, the pollen sticks. A tube starts growing out of the grain. The tube stretches down through the thin strand of silk. On and

on it grows. The long tube of pollen pushes
into the ovule at the end of the strand of silk.
When the pollen reaches the ovule, the ovule
has been pollinated. Pollinated ovules are
called seeds, or kernels.

Pollen lands on leaves, and silks, and baby ears.
When it sticks to a silk, it grows.

The pollinated ovules grow inside the ear. The ear grows bigger. The plant builds a stretchy coat around each seed. The plant begins to fill the kernels with starch and sugar.

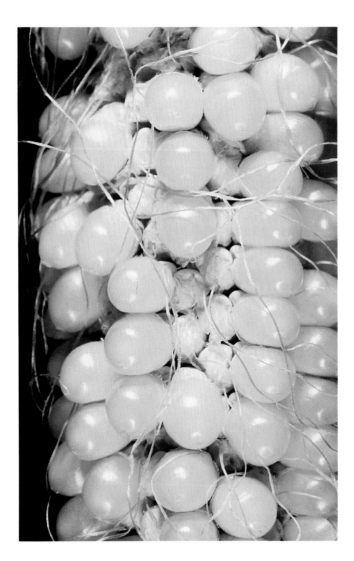

Some ovules on this ear of corn did not grow. Only pollinated ovules grow.

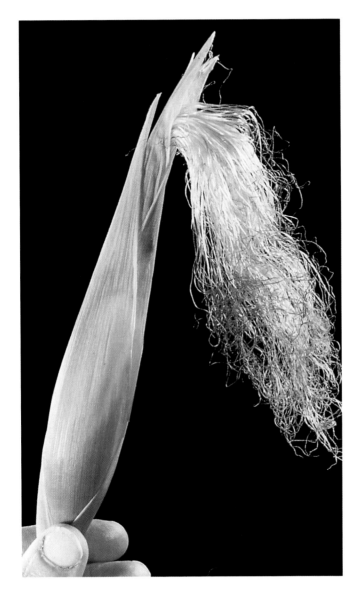

This ear is too small to be picked. It will grow to be more than twice this long.

If you picked the ear now and tried to pop the kernels, they wouldn't pop. The kernels need to keep growing.

Chapter 5

There are many different kinds of popcorn plants. What do we call a plant that's a mix of its parents?

Making New Kinds of Seeds

If a popcorn kernel is planted, it can grow into a new popcorn plant. If the ovule and the pollen came from the same kind of popcorn plant, the baby plant will look just like its parents. But sometimes pollen from one kind of popcorn lands on the silk of a different kind of popcorn plant. Then the baby plant is a mix of its parents. It is called a hybrid (HYE-brid).

Hybrids happen in two ways. Sometimes wind blows pollen from one kind of popcorn plant to another. Other times a farmer moves the pollen.

Wind can scatter pollen from plant to plant.

A farmer can use a bag to collect pollen from a corn plant.

The farmer puts the pollen of one plant on the sticky silk of another kind of popcorn plant. This farmer has a plan. The farmer wants to make a new hybrid that is different from the old popcorn plants.

A farmer may already grow one kind of popcorn with kernels that pop extra fast and extra big. The farmer may grow another kind of popcorn with bright purple kernels. The farmer can move the pollen from one kind of plant to the ears of the other kind of plant. Then the kernels that grow on the new plant are hybrid seeds. If the hybrid seeds are planted, they will grow into new kinds of plants. Some of the new plants' kernels will be bright purple. They will pop extra fast *and* extra big, too!

Popcorn kernels come in many different colors. A farmer might name this purple hybrid "Royal Purple Poppers."

Chapter 6

This popcorn ear is fully grown. Its stalk and leaves have dried up and died. How do farmers pick the corn from the stalks?

The Kernel Goes "Pop!"

By fall, each kernel of popcorn is packed full of starch and sugar. The ear of popcorn is fully grown. The seed coat around each kernel begins to dry out. As the coat dries, it gets hard. The hard coat keeps the seed inside it safe.

The popcorn plant has done its job of making seeds. The plant dies. Farmers pick the corn from the stalks. This is called harvesting. Harvesting is done with giant machines. The machines also tear the husks from the ears and pull the kernels free. The seeds are ready to plant. Or they are ready to be popped.

These farmers are harvesting their corn crop.

Farmers save some seeds to plant next year. The rest of the kernels are the popcorn that we eat. They are sealed in tight packages. This keeps the seed coats hard and dry.

Farmers can feed corn stalks to their pigs and cows.

Dried popcorn kernels are harder than most kinds of corn kernels.

Most corn kernels dry all the way through, but a tiny bit of water is left inside popcorn seeds. If you make a popcorn kernel very, very hot, the water left inside it will boil. When water boils, it turns to steam. A little bit of water boils up into a lot of steam. There is much more steam than will fit inside the hard, dry coat of a popcorn kernel. The steam builds up, until finally the kernel explodes with a "pop!"

Popped popcorn is always white, because every kernel's center is white. When popcorn kernels pop, they turn inside out.

The kernel is blown inside out by the explosion. Its white starchy center is on the outside. Once a kernel has popped, it can never grow into a plant. That is fine. Farmers saved plenty of other seeds to plant next spring.

There will be another crop ready next fall. So you can enjoy every tasty bite of your popcorn.

Fields of popcorn are grown all over the world.

On Sharing a Book

As you know, adults greatly influence a child's attitude toward reading. When a child sees you read, or when you share a book with a child, you're sending a message that reading is important. Show the child that reading a book together is important to you. Find a comfortable, quiet place. Turn off the television and limit other distractions like telephone calls.

Be prepared to start slowly. Take turns reading parts of this book. Stop and talk about what you're reading. Talk about the photographs. You may find that much of the shared time is spent discussing just a few pages. This discussion time is valuable for both of you, so don't move through the book too quickly. If the child begins to lose interest, stop reading. Continue sharing the book at another time. When you do pick up the book again, be sure to revisit the parts you have already read. Most importantly, enjoy the book!

Be a Vocabulary Detective

You will find a word list on page 5. Words selected for this list are important to the understanding of the topic of this book. Encourage the child to be a word detective and search for the words as you read the book together. Talk about what the words mean and how they are used in the sentence. Do any of these words have more than one meaning? You will find these words defined in a glossary on page 46.

What about Questions?

Use questions to make sure the child understands the information in this book. Here are some suggestions:

> What did this paragraph tell us? What does this picture show? What do you think we'll learn about next? Where do popcorn plants grow? Do popcorn plants grow wild? How is popcorn similar to other grass plants people eat? How is it different? How does a popcorn kernel grow? How does a popcorn plant make its own food? How does pollen move from one plant to another? Why does popcorn pop? What is your favorite part of this book? Why?

If the child has questions, don't hesitate to respond with questions of your own like: What do *you* think? Why? What is it that you don't know? If the child can't remember certain facts, turn to the index.

Introducing the Index

The index is an important learning tool. It helps readers get information quickly without searching throughout the whole book. Turn to the index on page 48. Choose an entry, such as *roots,* and ask the child to use the index to find out how deep a popcorn plant's roots grow. Repeat this exercise with as many entries as you like. Ask the child to point out the differences between an index and a glossary. (The index helps readers find information quickly, while the glossary tells readers what words mean.)

All the World in Metric!

Although our monetary system is in metric units (based on multiples of 10), the United States is one of the few countries in the world that does not use the metric system of measurement. Here are some conversion activities you and the child can do using a calculator:

WHEN YOU KNOW:	MULTIPLY BY:	TO FIND:
miles	1.609	kilometers
feet	0.3048	meters
inches	2.54	centimeters
gallons	3.787	liters
pounds	0.454	kilograms

Activities

1) Collect dried seeds from different kinds of plants: corn kernels, rice grains, apple seeds, and melon seeds, for example. Look closely at the seeds. Notice that they have different shapes and colors. Now make a collage with the seeds. Spread a layer of glue on a piece of stiff paper or cardboard. Place the seeds on top of the glue in a pattern that you like, then let the glue dry.

2) A fun and easy experiment will prove that moisture makes popcorn pop. Put a handful of popcorn in a shallow bowl. Leave the popcorn uncovered for two to three days to dry. Remove half the kernels and try to pop them. Do they pop? Put the rest of the dried kernels in a jar with a teaspoon of water. Cover the jar and wait two days. Then try to pop these kernels. Do they pop better than the dried kernels did?
Note: Adult supervision is necessary.

3) Popcorn plants have been around for thousands of years. Try to imagine how people popped popcorn before there were stoves or microwave ovens. Go to the library and find out how people discovered that popcorn will pop.

Glossary

carbon dioxide (dy-AHK-side)—a part of air that plants use to make food

chlorophyll (KLOR-uh-fihl)—the green substance found in a plant that makes food for the plant

corn silk—the threads at the end of an ear of corn

hybrid (HYE-brid)—a plant whose parents are two different kinds of plants

minerals (MIN-ur-uhls)—things found in the soil that are not plants or animals

nodes—thick places on a corn stalk from which leaves grow

ovules (AHV-yoolz)—baby seeds on an ear of corn

pollen—yellow powder from a male flower

pollinated—pollen has been carried from the male flower to the female flower so kernels can form

stalks (STAWKS)—the main stems of corn plants

starch—a food made by plants

tassel (TASS-uhl)—the male flower of a popcorn plant

Index

Pages listed in **bold** type refer to photographs.